The Little Book

Austin Winchester

ISBN 978-1-63903-784-1 (paperback)
ISBN 978-1-63903-785-8 (digital)

Copyright © 2021 by Austin Winchester

All rights reserved. No part of this publication may be reproduced, distributed, or transmitted in any form or by any means, including photocopying, recording, or other electronic or mechanical methods without the prior written permission of the publisher. For permission requests, solicit the publisher via the address below.

Christian Faith Publishing, Inc.
832 Park Avenue
Meadville, PA 16335
www.christianfaithpublishing.com

Printed in the United States of America

Chapter 1

TO THOSE CALLED AND sanctified by truth and to the body and blood of Christ, in which all truth resides, blessings of peace, grace, mercy, and divine revelation unto you.

To those seeking truth and not yet attaining it, let Christ reign in your mind and be etched on your heart. For I once was numbered amongst the sinners. I pray that your mind will come to know peace…true peace. Never allow a passing second of ease from your internal torment, caused by your personal passions and desires, that you may eventually know Christ, even now. I urge you to crucify your flesh and partake of the body and blood of Christ Jesus in whom all life resides and in who alone has all wisdom, knowledge, and perfect understanding of all things. Whoever does not partake of the body and blood of Christ has no life in him, and he who partakes falsely is guilty of the body and blood.

Nonetheless, blessings of mercy and grace be unto you. I pray for peace for you have no peace, as you are of your father, the evil one. This is why you are of your father, called the devil and Satan, because you are in and of the world. For what is written by John in his gospel, let it be true, *"I will no longer talk much with you, for the ruler of this world is coming, and he has nothing in Me"* (John 14:30 NKJV). He adds in 1 John 2:15–17, *"Do not love the world or the things in the world. If anyone loves the world, the love of the Father is not in him. For all that is in the world—the lust of the flesh, the lust of the eyes, and pride of life—is not of the Father but is of the world. And the world is passing away and the lust of it; but he who does the will of God abides forever."* Paul says in Galatians 5:9, *"A little leaven leavens the whole lump."* And as the leaven leavens the whole lump, you cannot be pious, apart from the righteousness of Christ. As a slave to sin, remember that a son abides in the house forever. Therefore, let there be hope for you for *who the Son sets free is free indeed* (John 8:36). Amen.

Chapter 2

IF LOCKED IN THE futility of one's own mind, how can man hope for a chance at reasonable notion? We are blinded by the darkness of our own intellect. What is true? Who is true? For what cause has uniformity become uniform or is it structured chaos? Chaos driven manually is a chaos unto which logic may be applied and creates a universe where we may come to think free thought. Patterns can be found in infinity, but so can everlasting disarray. Therefore, one may conclude that reason cannot reason at all, and the only true truth lies within structured spontaneity. Are these things not written in the Gospel according to Saint John where our Lord says, *"The wind blows where it wishes, and you hear the sound of it, but cannot tell where it comes from and where it goes. So is everyone who is born of the Spirit"* (John 3:8). Paul says in his epistle to the Corinthians, *"For 'who has known the mind of the Lord that he may instruct Him?' But we have the mind of Christ"* (1 Corinthians 2:16), and the array of thought outside the mind of self, thus truth lies in posterity.

For mind to prove reason would be for opinion to prove truth or instinct to overthrow instinct. It would be likewise to say that darkness can overthrow darkness or light to light. Light overcomes darkness, but not darkness to light. Light in fact does not need to overtake darkness, for that would imply worthiness or at least admirable resistance, but all it needs to do is be present in the midst of darkness, and darkness is no longer in its midst. Darkness simply ceases to be when it is before light. Likewise, reason ceases to be without posterity, and reason cannot exist without mind.

Our entire thought process is founded upon mathematics. Everything we were taught is derived from the most simple of equations and compounded by experience and profession. We base everything we know of the natural universe off a system of understanding. According to what is one plus two equals three (1 + 2 = 3)? By what proof does math remain practical? What of division by zero (0) and other impossible possibilities? Why then should it be practical to base an entire system of logic in science on a system where impossibility is possible? We simply disregard it and look at what does indeed make sense. Why should I disregard such irrefutable evidence against such a way of thought? Who is to say what is what since we are without reason, except by means of justification of a flawed system because we fail to explain an inconsistency by stating it just cannot work for the sake of the rest of the system working?

It is ironic that we are able to "practically apply" mathematics to the natural world and attempt to explain it by means of an unjustified system. The world of mathematics is always supporting new perspectives of old equations and finding proofs of new truths, but when it comes to justifying its own foundation, it cannot succeed in doing so. Even greater so, if I may state, that it chooses to label things as "undefined" to mask a lie as a truth that is within its own laws in order to ignore and justify itself. Where is its witness? What proves math and science? It's quite the contrary. We have created a system that relies upon itself to stand as truth. We have declared a monarch to be just, but on what merit? Because the monarch says so? Paul strictly warned against this in his second epistle to the church of Corinth, saying, *"For we dare not class ourselves or compare ourselves with those who commend themselves. But they, measuring themselves by themselves, and comparing themselves among themselves, are not wise"* (2 Corinthians 10:12).

Say there is a group of people with a dialect that never determined left as left and right as right. Said people could then not distinguish their left foot from their right foot. How would such people then make an inference to an injury to their left or right foot? By default, these people would need to learn environmental forms of distinguishing the difference of one side of their body from the other.

THE LITTLE BOOK

Earth is a globe. There are magnetic poles that are observed but do not "need" to be proven because they are constant. It is objective to the situation for where the problem is based. These people would most likely identify with worldwide direction. Whether that be with certain landmarks in different locations in the surrounding area or by actual magnetic direction, it doesn't really matter. By default, there is a north, south, east, and west. These people would need to communicate that their injured foot, being left or right, is north, south, east, or west (these directions do not have to be called that but for our sakes, we shall continue calling them that). For example, "My *easternmost* foot is injured." You may see where obvious problems would arise in this. One would need to know his own position and facing direction relative to the earth at all times. This is not a practical way of identifying one's own injury, but it is a more than practical way of identifying an object in a specific location in accordance to the world. The North Pole is the north and the south the south.

To remain truly intellectually honest, this is how we must think. Why is this so? To say "my left or right" is a selfish statement, but to say "my northernmost or southernmost" is a worldwide constant and pertains to the earth as the actual object, but the current space it occupies. *Left* and *right* are crutch words for the thinking mind. One may as well say, "I am smart." To whom or what are you actually smart? To yourself? Or because according to another mind, you are considered smart? To what measure? In which matter? Is it conditional? Just as *left* is conditioned to be *right* because if I look in a mirror, left becomes right, to which does truth lie? What do I observe about myself in the mirror or in the fact that I am positive my perception of left and right is the true left and right? A man looks into the mirror and observes himself. When he walks away, he immediately forgets his natural face—that is, the truth. This truth is that while observing yourself in a natural manner, it must be in the opposite of what you experience. Thus, when we observe ourselves, we see something different than what we feel. And while observing, we experience that which we cannot feel. This is to say that we cannot completely know ourselves without using an outside source, which tells us what we are in truth, yet the opposite of what we think we are. Our Lord tells His disciples, *"If anyone desires to come after Me, let him deny himself, and take up his cross, and follow Me"* (Matthew 16:24). He says in John 12:24, *"Most assuredly, I say to you, unless a grain of wheat falls into the ground and dies, it remains alone; but if it dies, it produces much grain."* Until we receive cognition of who we are in the mirror, we, by default, cannot be complete.

This leads me to the fact that when considering identifying truth, truth lies in posterity. This is the difference between selfishness and selflessness. To say left or right is selfish, but to say northernmost or southernmost is selfless. This is the difference between instinct and mind. Instinct tells us we have a sex drive so we need to have sex now in order to appease it or that I must protect my life at all costs in order to continue my life. Mind tells us that we are married and away from home so we cannot have sex. The mind says to protect my wife or close friend's life above my own because I love them. Instinct says that I must protect my life over my wife or close friend in order to continue appeasing my instinct. The mind says that I care for my wife or my close friend too much in order for them to die, so I will place their needs above my own. Our Lord says in John 15:13, *"Greater love has no one than this, than to lay down one's life for his friends."* Now the *mind* in this sense is just the deciding factor for reasoning between two options: for the benefit of others or the benefit of myself, or the consciousness (this can be corrupt [when corrupt, it is more numb, than disintegrated] or pure). When thinking of such things, it is also important to note that instinct is the preservation of the flesh and mind (when undefiled) is the consideration of the greater good of nature, others, or self. Paul confirms these things by saying:

> *For I delight in the law of God according to the inward man. But I see another law in my members, warring against the law of my mind, and bringing me into captivity to the law of sin which is in my members. O wretched man that I am! Who will deliver me from this body of death? I thank God—through Jesus Christ our Lord! So then, with the*

mind I myself serve the law of God, but with the flesh the law of sin. (Romans 7:22–25)

Thus, it can be stated that the love of my fellow man preserves others; therefore, love is the pilot of the mind. Instinct is always considering how to protect myself in order to satisfy the instinct. Therefore, it can be stated that fear is the pilot of instinct (flesh). Love considers posterity, and fear considers self. How then may one rightfully say, "It makes sense to me" and consider himself correct? The correct statement must state, "It makes sense to the whole." This is because it considers what is correct according to truth, which lies in posterity, which lies in love. Therefore, instinct lies in the flesh and the flesh in fear. Fear in turn either makes one fight or fly, meaning it denies its very own demise. A proverb says, *"Do not be afraid of sudden terror"* (Proverbs 3:25). How then may we choose to be suddenly afraid without the transforming and renewing of our minds in peace and love?

Now I am not saying that proof through arithmetic is false because it is not, but what I am saying is to base an entire line of thinking on such a thing as mathematics is foolishness. A mind cannot fully know another mind, *"For 'who has known the mind of the Lord that he may instruct him?' But we have the mind of Christ"* (1 Corinthians 2:16). Therefore, instinct cannot understand a concept such as love rendering the body powerless in the precincts of reason, posterity, and truth. For as it is written by Saint John in his first epistle to the saints, *"There is no fear in love; but perfect love casts out fear, because fear involves torment. But he who fears has not been made perfect in love"* (1 John 4:18).

The mind is not inherently selfish but is the will to reason and the unadulterated consciousness for the distinction between good and bad works, while the body (self, the flesh) is inherently selfish and exists only for advantage gained and self-preservation. Of this matter, Paul writes, *"Therefore do not let sin reign in your mortal body, that you should obey it in its lusts"* (Romans 6:12).

Chapter 3

THE SPIRIT IS THE thing that ties principles and powers to physical reality and the reality of the mind. The trinity is found representing this ideology: the Father, *"But of that day and hour no one knows, not even the angels in heaven, nor the Son, but only the Father"* (Mark 13:32); the Son, *"For we do not have a High Priest who cannot sympathize with our weaknesses, but was in all* points *tempted as* we are, *yet without sin"* (Hebrews 4:15); and of the Spirit, *"And it shall come to pass in the last days, says God, that I will pour out of My Spirit on all flesh; your sons and daughters shall prophesy, your young men shall see visions, and your old men shall dream dreams"* (Acts 2:17). Matthew 10:19–20 says, *"But when they deliver you up, do not worry about how or what you should speak. For it will be given to you in that hour what you should speak; for it is not you who speak, but the Spirit of your Father who speaks in you."*

In the beginning, God made man in His image and according to Their likeness, for all things are of Him, to Him, and through Him, for He was crucified before the foundations of the world. So of the Godhead, we are made one as the Father of the mind, the Son of the flesh, and His Holy Spirit of the spirit. We are the triune divine partakers of God as He is with Himself, and us by Him in Him. This is why blasphemy of the Spirit is unforgivable because a conscientious decision must be made to go against that mark of God within us and in Him; that is, the inherent good thing that resides inside of us that is holy and pure and convicts us of sin. When the mind actively follows the spirit, the flesh is then crucified according to the movement of the spirit in our minds. The Spirit of God gave the

Son of God power (not that the Son does not have power Himself, but that He became a Son of Man and needed the Spirit to do the good works of His Father in heaven) to act out not according to His will, but the will of His Father who is in heaven, that is, the one who makes decisions, for, *"'I am going to the Father,' for My Father is greater than I"* (John 14:28).

The Father is greater than the Son, and the Son has the Holy Spirit of His Father. The Spirit is Holy and pure, as is the Father and the Son, but the Spirit is the good promise given to the sons of men that we may walk holy and upright as God is holy and upright in all of His ways. Thus, the likeness of God in us is that of the making of us triune. If one part of the trinity in ourselves fails its purpose according to our own lusts, then we become partakers of unrighteousness to walk according to the father of lies and partake of his defiled resources. Then as Jesus was born, as it was, possible to sin, we are also made possible to sin, but as we were born into sin, we must regain righteousness by His Spirit according to the sacrifice of the Son's flesh. In God is love, for He is love, for there was always three of Him to love from the beginning. When the Son became sin for us, He was declared holy and righteous by God for mercy was shown to men who had not the Spirit of God. God's love was affirmed, and by Him our love is confirmed in Him by Him. God had to be made with the possibility of sin in order for His love within Himself to be loving of Himself [not to say God needs us, for God has no need for flesh, but only that He was crucified from the beginning, so His love has always been affirmed apart from us, but instead, we need Him.]

Paul writes, *"Do not be deceived, God is not mocked; for whatever a man sows, that he will also reap"* (Galatians 6:7). God sows into us His righteousness that we may be one with Him as He is with Himself. This atonement makes His flesh—and thus, our flesh—the mediator of reality. We (mankind) are made of spirit, mind, and flesh in the likeness of our God in heaven who is also spirit, mind, and flesh all working according to a single will. His perfection is made evident to all sons of men in that we are made perfect in Him. It is written by James, known as the brother of the Christ, *"As the body without the spirit is dead, so faith without works is dead"* (James 2:26).

Chapter 4

IT IS IMPOSSIBLE TO partake in any good work without actively partaking in faith. What is the advantage of the good work compared to the bad work? The bad work here would be selfishness at the expense of another. The good work is selflessness with negative connotation toward the source of good. Faith can be said to be the substance of things hoped for. If this is the case, then how may any good action derived outside of self-sufficiency be anything outside of faith? Any action taken for the positive effect of another, disregarding my own self, is an action of faith. The opposite can also be said. Faith can also be the lack of action taken for any positive or negative outcome. Faith is the reliable factor that states if an action be taken (or not taken), we have a hope or an assurance that the intended outcome will ensue, whether it be positive or negative. It is impossible to partake in a negative (morally bad) action and hope for a positive outcome for all parties affected. Thus, we may conclude that an action taken by any individual can lead to good or bad results due to intention. Not to say that positive intentions with a bad result is good, but only that time and chance happens to all and the intended original result was purposed from a pure conscience.

Saint James writes on faith as such in his holy epistle to the brethren:

> "What does it profit, my brethren, if someone says he has faith but does not have works? Can faith save him? If a brother or sister is naked and destitute of daily food, and one of you says to them, 'Depart in

> *peace, be warmed and filled,' but you do not give them the things which are needed for the body, what does it profit? Thus, also faith by itself, if it does not have works, is dead. But someone will say, 'You have faith, and I have works.' Show me your faith without your works, and I will show you my faith by my works."* (James 2:14–18)

And again

> *"Was not Abraham our father justified by works when he offered Isaac his son on the altar?"* (James 2:21)

Faith by itself is dead apart from works because faith is believing in something while you enact upon nothing. When enacting upon nothing, you are openly declaring there is a promise of something, but true faith lies in a coexistence of laborers (whether that is between you and God or between the brethren) in hope of receiving nothing (or at the very least, righteousness). Faith encompasses all things. A world where the absence of faith is impossible shows us that even in doubt, we have faith in a negative outcome. Free will is truly free from being deterministic, but not free in that every decision has a set consequence. These outcomes could be determined by every action taken throughout history by not only humans, but by the seemingly small and/or insignificant life as well. Every action has a chance to be one thing or another (in simplicity), but nothing is actually impossible nor not all things possible.

In a universe where God rules and God is all good, then people must be given freedom of choice in order to secure the goodness of God. In a universe where there is no God, then there is no objective sense of moral value in accordance to the motives of the heart. There would merely be chance and no opportunity to be given the notion of even hating God. For if all is chance with no sense of higher guidance, we are always succumbing to instinct to fulfill our needs. Selfishness would no longer be considered evil. No one would so much as bat an eye (positively or negatively) at the moral value of any given person for any action taken by anyone (except that of personal affliction), for it would be born of advantage gained, the only known desire of any man (the flesh).

It is only possible in a world with no God that life is determined. Every decision that can be made has been made or will be made, which means we are slaves to the universe and time. However, in a world with a just, all good, and merciful God, free will is required. We make decisions according to our own merit, yet we have already made every decision that will be made and has been made. This is not according to God's will, but according to our own. Everything is determined, yet not everything is desired. Paul writes to Rome, *"For whom He foreknew, He also predestined* to be *conformed to the image of His Son, that He might be the firstborn among many brethren. Moreover whom He predestined, these He also called; whom He called, these He also justified; and whom He justified, these He also glorified"* (Romans 8:29–30. Peter also writes in his second epistle, *"But, beloved, do not forget this one thing, that with the Lord one day* is *as a thousand years, and a thousand years as one day. The Lord is not slack concerning* His *promise, as some count slackness, but is longsuffering toward us, not willing that any should perish but that all should come to repentance"* (2 Peter 3:8–10). In all of this, however, the beginning is preordained and the end is set, but we as saints should be as Peter says in 2 Peter 3:12, *"looking for and hastening the coming of the day of God, because of which the heavens will be dissolved, being on fire, and the elements will melt with fervent heat."*

In these three things, the preeminence of reason exists: space, time, and harmony. Just as space cannot be perceived without time, nor time be evaluated apart from space, neither of these things exist without harmony. The harmony of the universe is exactly what makes space interact with time as it does. Without harmony, there is nothing. Through harmony, creation is able to be. Aristotle explains *nothing* as, *"what rocks dream of."* We cannot begin to fully understand nothing because there has always been something. As long as there is something, nothing cannot exist. Nothing could have never actually existed because it knows not time nor space; therefore, it simply isn't.

Just as God is the "I AM," Christ Jesus always was and always will be. If Christ Jesus always was, then there is life eternal. Eternal life is not nothing. Life eternal is not just something, it is all things that must be. To not be is for being to be not, and to be not is forever for it cannot be. Therefore, it never will be. Christ Jesus is simply the *"[visible] image of the invisible God"* (Colossians 1:15). Since He is the "I AM," then the Word can only be the flesh manifest for He said, *"Let there be,"* and there was. All things have not always been, but He has. Therefore, all things are made for the glory of the image of Christ and created to be a suitable habitation for His presence. We, the vessels of His glory, are partakers of His divine nature. We will be like Him, yet not Him.

Life is the most valuable gift of all, seeing as to how something must always be better than nothing. It is never merited to take one's own life (unless divinely ordained, as we observe in the story of Samson) or another's for we know the hope of the glory we shall inherit, but the world does not. Whether in hardship or in luxury, in pain or in pleasure, in comfort or in strife, in war or in peace, in heaven or in hell, life is always worth living no matter the valley because something is always better than nothing. There will never be nothing so God's justice must be in play. While God's justice must happen, we were never purposed for hell for God prepared hell for the devil and his angels. As it is written, *"Then He will also say to those on the left hand, 'Depart from Me, you cursed, into the everlasting fire prepared for the devil and his angels.'"* (Matthew 25:41)

Satan invented lies and birthed unrighteousness. Since there is no comfort in strife, since strife has no place in God, and since carnal pleasure knows no end, the birth pangs never leave *Sheol*. If we have communion with the devil called Satan, we do not know God because we have the love of the world in us, for Satan is the ruler of this world, and we chose to reject Christ's hand in marriage and spread our evil seed, as Jezebel would have it. While for us sons of men, we have this hope and assurance of origin, *"Then the King will say to those on His right hand, 'Come, you blessed of My Father, inherit the kingdom prepared for you from the foundation of the world"* (Matthew 25:34). John Milton writes, *"That with reiterated crimes he* (Satan) *might heap on himself damnation, while he sought evil to others; and enraged might see how all his malice served but to bring forth infinite goodness, grace, and mercy shown on man by him seduced."*

So as all things have been created with the same harmony of God's life because in Him is preeminence in all things. Of this matter, Christ speaks in Matthew 6:28–30, *"Consider the lilies of the field, how they grow: they neither toil nor spin; and yet I say to you that even Solomon in all his glory was not arrayed like one of these. Now if God so clothes the grass of the field, which today is, and tomorrow is thrown into the oven, will He not much more clothe you, O you of little faith?"*—And by Luke, *"Then, as He was now drawing near the descent of the Mount of Olives, the whole multitude of the disciples began to rejoice and praise God with a loud voice for all the mighty works they had seen, saying: '"Blessed is the King who comes in the name of the Lord!" Peace in heaven and glory in the highest!' And some of the Pharisees called to Him from the crowd, 'Teacher, rebuke Your disciples.' But He answered and said to them, 'I tell you that if these should keep silent, the stones would immediately cry out.'"* (Luke 19:37–40)

If in Him is the preeminence, then Adam was not the first man. Christ Jesus was the first man. So after Adam was I born, and in Christ Adam was born, I am born into a fallen world, brought on by the sin of Adam and restored to life in Christ Jesus, which was lost, that which was from the beginning. Perfect, blessed, whole, holy, never-ending life, always present, yet having passed away and yet to come, Jesus is the hope of all mankind and the very faith we hold on to. Paul writes to Timothy, his son in the faith, in his second letter, saying, *"This is a faithful saying: for if we died with* Him, *we shall also live with* Him. *If we endure, we shall also reign with* Him. *If we deny* Him, *He also will deny us. If we are faithless, He remains faithful; He cannot deny Himself"* (2 Timothy 2:11–13).

Chapter 5

UNDERSTANDING AND AGREEMENT SHOULD not be made equal. Understanding is the measure of comprehension, and agreement would make both sides correct. Instead, I would insist that to win an argument would be to substantiate to the opposing party your view to make them question themselves as to why they cannot answer the same question(s) and not contradict themselves, opening their own mind to the objective truth and realizing their own fault themselves. This is the only way a mind is changed and an argument won. You must humble yourself to trust in the intellect of your opponent to make the correct conscious decision. Understand and empathize because both parties cannot be correct. To say this would be to subject truth to mere opinion and to make reality whatever anyone wants it to be. This would be madness, and the structure of the universe requires singularity. Truth must stand on its own to be truth or it is not truth at all (God is truth, but He bears witness of Himself on three parts). One must also understand that not all can grasp truth. Do not be comfortable with ignorance. Instead, accept them as fools because you presented to them the proper tools for revelation, yet they rejected them. Therefore, those who humble themselves shall inherit the earth. God first told His servant Job, *"Now prepare yourself like a man"* (Job 38:3). Then He said to His servant and high apostle Paul, *"When I was a child, I spoke as a child, I understood as a child, I thought as a child; but when I became a man, I put away childish things"* (1 Corinthians 13:11). Therefore, the true measure of man is understanding and having "ears to hear."

Subjective truth is like a sprout found within somebody's lawn that is constantly growing just to be cut down again and again. Conversely, objective truth is like one of those sprouts that keeps growing out of sight, away from the supervision of a landlord. This sprout is permitted to keep growing by the resources that give it life into a mighty oak. Then all the birds of the air may make their nest in it and perch proudly. Meanwhile, the sprout in the lawn is under destructive influence, unless it is determined to be the "proper" or "desired" sprout. In which case, it is continually trimmed and hedged that it may fit the landlord's criteria or it is cut down and replaced. Never allowed to grow, it is cut once too much growth is observed. Metaphorically, we are tended by God in His garden called Eden, naturally tamed by His love, His life. While in God's garden, where Christ is Lord, we are incorruptibly, immaculately, impeccably hedged—not by man-made tools, which destroy what is already growing in an attempt to perfect that which grew imperfectly, but of God, the original plant withers and dies, just as the fig which bore no fruit. And we are planted anew and grow according to His divine will into the desired shape, height, and form. This way the desired birds, which may not have had a proper home before, may now perch peacefully and rest in their designed optimal home. This optimal growth of us in God's garden ensures us that we are never forsaken.

I speak to you not in human terms, but in faith because of the strength of the grace of God in His body, the church. Jesus spoke in parables, according to the flesh in human terms, that the scripture should be fulfilled saying, *"Seeing they may see and not perceive, and hearing they may hear and not understand; lest they should turn, and their sins be forgiven them"* (Mark 4:12). Jude writes in his epistle, *"To those who are called, sanctified by God the Father, and preserved in Jesus Christ"* (Jude 1:1), *"on some have compassion"* (Jude 1:22), and to make a distinction, *"save with fear, pulling them out of the fire, hating even the garment defiled by the flesh"* (Jude 1:23) By necessity, we as a people must know that a distinction is to be made from person to person. Fear abounds more clearly on some and compassion on others. How much more does this imply? We are not to subject ourselves to falsehoods, but to instead convince others of the truth by making a distinction by who they were created to be. Paul writes to the church of Rome, *"For the gifts and calling of God are irrevocable"* (Romans 11:29). We are to realize that many are presupposed to gravitate toward certain behavior, as opposed to the thing that opposes themselves. As Jesus says to *"Love your neighbor as you love yourself"* (Matthew 22:39), we know that we are to find who each of us is made to be in God and, by the Spirit, make a discernment on how to speak and show mercy on them. The Lord said, *"Father forgive them, for they know not what they do"* (Luke 23:34) and *"Do not worry about how or what you should speak. For it will be given to you in that hour what you should speak"* (Matthew 10:19).

It is commonly known to us all is that people will not always listen to or be convinced by what convinces others. This is why making distinction and recognizing individualization is of utmost importance, yet it is not about us. This does not change the truth or the message presented, but instead relays the same message to all, making the distinction. Aristotle writes, *"We must be able to employ persuasion, just as strict reasoning can be employed, on opposite sides of a question, not in order that we may in practice employ it in both ways (for we must not make people believe what is wrong), but in order that we may see clearly what the facts are, and that, if another man argues unfairly, we on our part may be able to confute him."* Apostle Paul said to Titus, his son in the spirit, *"Holding fast the faithful word as he has been taught, that he may be able, by sound doctrine, both to exhort and convict those who contradict"* (Titus 1:9). Not all can make this distinction, but as it was said by Him in which truth resides, *"He who has ears to hear, let him hear!"* (Matthew 11:15). Aristotle writes, *"They will often have allowed themselves to be so much influenced by feelings of friendship or hatred or self-interest that they lose any clear vision of the truth and have their judgement obscured by considerations of personal pleasure or pain."*

The law of human nature essentially comes down to one man trying to justify himself without actually looking at objective standards, which are found in the moral law or *"law of fair play,"* as C. S. Lewis likened to it. We as people like to view ourselves as the exception to every standard because our particular case is special and we are no longer within the bounds of this law, which is shown to be true through empirical evidence of the people surrounding us daily. The doctrine of moral law is for the majority throughout the world among the educated and uneducated. To those with and without understanding, an exclusive universal truth through philosophical means and cannot be understood by physical, only metaphysical, observation (not to say morality does not sometimes manifest itself physically, only that morality is, in its purity, metaphysical). The fact that such a thing exists and anti-practiced through acts of subconscious objective understanding points out that there must be some sort of "mind" beyond the flesh.

This law is observed in tribes and tongues in every known culture across the world. The truth can be twisted but never flayed. Take for example, a culture in which deceit is a sign of power and wisdom where you rise the ranks of politics in your tribe because you are the best liar of them all. People may argue different cultures contrive different morals to find the most effective way to evolve and survive. Such blathering is nonsensical. A tribe in which effective deceit means a rise to power only proves that looking out for yourself instinctively at the expense of others makes you nothing less than scandalous. Negative emotion is the most likely response to such an event. The deceived may make statements such as "It is his right" or "He bested me," but this is only speech pertaining to the social event and their nationalist mind, an attempt to justify the natural negative response within the standards of their community. The outlying fact remains that the man does not make the action taken to be good, only advantageous. There is a very large difference between the two that can seem difficult to distinguish in intuition but very easily distinguished through theoretical deduction of the *a priori* or preexisting terms of knowledge, which exist purely whether observed or not. Because instinct is concerned with being advantageous and not good but still knows there to be a distinctive right and wrong is clear evidence that justice is not determined by means of what is fair, but by means of what is good because we always (by instinct) make ourselves out to be justified knowing that we are in fact not justified. Through much training of this instinctual intuition of skewed justice, we can deceive ourselves to "know" that we are justified, although in objectivity we are not justified.

Plato writes in his dialogue, *Republic*, *"He who is of a calm and happy nature will hardly feel the pressure of age, but he who is of the opposite disposition, youth and age are equally a burden."* Luke writes of Paul's account with Christ in the Acts of the Apostles, *"It is hard for you to kick against the goads"* (Acts 26:14). This is because there is in fact a law of morality that everybody knows exists yet choose to not follow it. After all their excuses, they find themselves just as burdened at the end of their life, as they were at the beginning, with no understanding as to why this is so.

Chapter 6

I HAVE OBSERVED A GREAT evil in the world. When a man reaches the point in which he decides—as a result of any given possible scenario, apart from sacrifice—that suicide is the greatest action with false hope of a better future, of nothingness, of heaven and hell, or of anything in between. This man either simply disregards his peers, friends, and family or places his own self above others. Suicide is an act of your taking on the role of God yourself, feeling the need or desire to take one's own life, apart from sacrifice. Paul writes to the Romans, *"Therefore He has mercy on whom He wills, and whom He wills He hardens. You will say to me then, 'Why does He still find fault? For who has resisted His will?' But indeed, O man, who are you to reply against God? Will the thing formed say to him who formed it, 'Why have you made me like this?' Does not the potter have power over the clay, from the same lump to make one vessel for honor and another for dishonor?"* (Romans 9:18–21). They go against their entire self, ignore—or better yet, subdue instinct—and crucify the spirit. The only thing that remains is their mind, which can make no decision other than self-expiration, being void of the very things tying the mind to reality.

The man who takes his own life participates in an ultimate act of cowardice because he makes himself his own god and finds no reason, by reason alone, within himself to continue in the life where his own person (a god) cannot fix the evils of his world by his own strength, thus he must escape. He realizes he has become a prisoner in his own world, not its master. The mind is incapable of good in and of itself, flesh is only capable of evil (apart from spirit), and spirit that begins as pure can be corrupted, which be the case of any man who finds nihilism to be the only possible solution. I must conclude that suicide is not only evil, but also a deception of one's own self into thinking it is actually doing itself good. The act is good subjectively and bad objectively, meaning that even when someone views suicide as being good, he is objectively stating in a skewed manner that God is all good, but man makes himself to be a god (and the ideology of God states that if He exists, then He must be all good), but his action is founded upon a lie. Therefore, he is not all good and is not actually representing his own ideals in a truthful manner, nor God's. He is blinded by the futility of his own mind, and darkened council (of which, is himself bearing witness of only himself, and his mind of only itself) has brought him to the most illogical logical solution. This is the total wisdom of humanity, for it is written, *"Then he threw down the pieces of silver in the temple and departed, and went and hanged himself"* (Matthew 27:5). The Preacher tells us, *"He who loves silver will not be satisfied with silver"* (Ecclesiastes 5:10).

The very moment suicide, apart from sacrifice, becomes an act of bravery is when ignorance truly supersedes foolishness. In ignorance, there is hope in the God of mercy. He understands our condition and is the High Priest who is able to sympathize with us, being tempted in all points (the lust of the eyes, the lust of the flesh, and the pride of life). This is observed in the gospels on that fateful day when Satan urged our High Priest to cast Himself off the pinnacle of the temple to display His divinity, to which case our Christ replies, *"It is written again, 'You shall not tempt the Lord your God'"* (Matthew 4:7). It is important now, brethren, that we understand through the righteousness of our Lord and Savior Jesus Christ, the Son of our Father in heaven, that we have become partakers of His divine nature. *"It is no longer I who live, but Christ who lives in me"* (Galatians 2:20) and *"Love has been perfected in us in this: That we may have boldness in the day of judgment; because as He is so are we in this world"* (1 John 4:17). We are new creations. Our old lives passed away, and all things made new. Being renewed by the transforming of our minds, we are not to be conformed to this world, but confirmed as bondservants of grace by the redemption blood of Jesus, the fruit of our lives being that of forgiveness, mercy, and righteous judgment. Inasmuch as Christ says, *"First remove the plank from your own eye, and then you will see clearly to remove the speck from your brother's eye"* (Matthew 7:5).

The mercy of God endures forever. It would be foolish to say that such ignorance is guaranteed to be condemned to hell. A man can believe in God and Jesus Christ, but only given up in a moment of weakness to the prince of iniquity in whom all lies originate for it is his own resource. Satan is the prerequisite to the son of perdition, so who is he to take the salvation of the Lord's anointed? Is he not also a prisoner of hell? Is God not the overseer of hell?

It is written in the Psalm of David:

> *"Where can I go from Your Spirit? Or where can I flee from Your presence? If I ascend into heaven, You* are *there; if I make my bed in hell, behold, You* are there. If *I take the wings of the morning, and dwell in the uttermost parts of the sea, even there Your hand shall lead me, and Your right hand shall hold me. If I say, 'Surely the darkness shall fall on me,' even the night shall be light about me; indeed, the darkness shall not hide from You, But the night shines as the day; the darkness and the light are both alike to You."* (Psalm 139:7–13)

Paul says to the church of Rome concerning salvation, *"Who shall bring a charge against God's elect? It is God who justifies"* (Romans 8:33).

I would like to hope that the man who takes his own life has a chance at heaven. To say otherwise would be for us to take a seat on God's throne, which is exactly what the fallen one attempted and failed to do. He was stricken with an eternity of weeping and gnashing of teeth in everlasting darkness, where the worm does not die and the fire rages with the wrath of its tormented. Such is the reward of a fool. Those who sin after they have come to the knowledge of truth, there remains no more sacrifice for sins. Paul the apostle wrote to the church of Galatia, *"But if, while we seek to be justified by Christ, we ourselves also are found sinners, is Christ therefore a minister of sin? Certainly not!"* (Galatians 2:17). Therefore, I say unto you, if I sin while under the knowledge-truth of Christ Jesus, I become a minister of foolishness instead of a beacon of righteousness. As the Lord Jesus Christ is perfect, we are all called to be the same for *"it is not I who live, but Christ who lives in me"* (Galatians 2:20) and *"Whoever abides in Him does not sin. Whoever sins has neither seen Him nor known Him"* (1 John 3:6). Saint Peter, the chosen rock on which the church was built after Christ, says in his first epistle, *"You shall be holy, for I am holy"* (1 Peter 1:16). Therefore, the sons of mercy shall inherit the earth and sit on their thrones of righteousness and glory to judge the angels and men, who revoked their rights to heavenly places by denying their very own divine nature.

Concerning the angels, Enoch laid judgment upon these as the Lord said to him, *"O righteous Enoch, thou scribe of righteousness: approach hither, and hear my voice. Go, say to the Watchers of heaven, who have sent thee to pray for them, 'You ought to pray for men, and not men for you'"* and *"But you from the beginning were made spiritual, possessing a life which is eternal, and not subject to death for ever."* These things are written in the epistle to the Hebrews, *"Are they not all ministering spirits sent forth to minister for those who will inherit salvation?"* (Hebrews 1:14) and again, *"For indeed He does not give aid to the angels, but He does give aid to the seed of Abraham"* (Hebrews 2:16). But we, as saints in Christ Jesus, sing a new song that the angels cannot know for it is written by John the Beloved.

> *"They sang as it were a new song before the throne, before the four living creatures, and the elders; and no one could learn that song except the hundred and forty-four thousand who were redeemed from the earth. These are the ones who were not defiled with women, for they are virgins. These are the ones who follow the Lamb wherever He goes. These were redeemed from among men, being firstfruits to God and to the Lamb. And in their mouth was found no*

deceit, for they are without fault before the throne of God." (Revelation 14:3–4)

I thank the one true God and His Son, whom He sent, that I may obtain mercy and be glorified with Him as He is with the Father. By the Spirit of truth and by that very same Spirit upon me, bring holy and righteous judgment upon Satan and his unholy angels and all workers of iniquity. Now Enoch, the seventh from Adam, also prophesied about these men, saying, *"Behold, the Lord comes with ten thousands of His saints, to execute judgment on all, to convict all who are ungodly among them of all their ungodly deeds which they have committed in an ungodly way, and of all the harsh things which ungodly sinners have spoken against Him"* (Jude 1:14–15). Now these are those who calumniate and turn the grace of the Lord our God in heaven, Father of all creation, and His Son Jesus the Christ into lasciviousness. These things are affirmed by Paul the apostle when he writes to the church of Corinth, saying, *"Do you not know that the saints will judge the world? And if the world will be judged by you, are you unworthy to judge the smallest matters? Do you not know that we shall judge angels? How much more, things that pertain to this life?"* (1 Corinthians 6:2–3). Our Lord Himself says concerning men, as it is written in the Gospel according to Saint Luke:

> *"And Jesus answered and said to him, 'Simon, I have something to say to you.' So he said, 'Teacher, say it.' 'There was a certain creditor who had two debtors. One owed five hundred denarii, and the other fifty. And when they had nothing with which to repay, he freely forgave them both. Tell Me, therefore, which of them will love him more?' Simon answered and said, 'I suppose* the *one whom he forgave more.' And He said to him, 'You have rightly judged.'"* (Luke 7:40–43)

So when we enter into unity with Christ Jesus the advocate, we may rightly judge, *"Do not judge according to appearance, but judge with righteous judgment"* (John 7:24). Who is more righteous than our Lord and Savior Jesus Christ? I say to you that no man is more righteous than He, and no man may even hope to attain righteousness without Him. So let us glorify God as He has bestowed the greatest power of all to men, who are sanctified by the washing and regeneration of His Holy Spirit, the power to forgive men of their sins, *"If you forgive the sins of any, their sins have been forgiven them; if you retain the sins of any, they have been retained"* (John 20:23).

Chapter 7

CONCERNING THE THINGS OF salvation and judgment, brethren, I feel that it is necessary for you to know the value of your life to God. He has our every hair numbered. He knows your substance before you were formed in your mother's womb. Perhaps God has failed you with regard to your anointing by His Holy Ghost. Does not God count you more worthy than many sparrows? I suppose He consecrated you as a priest and prophet before you were conceived. Are these things not written? Paul tells you that the saints will judge the angels. Having such a task on our hands, are we to annul the calling God has on our life? But I say to you, *"The gifts and calling of God are irrevocable"* (Romans 11:29). I am convinced that nothing can separate us from the love that God has for us, His children. While the love is never gone, God had favorites, *"Jacob I have loved, but Esau I have hated"* (Romans 9:13). Esau, being wicked, sold his entire birthright for a morsel of stew. I wish to add exactly as follows: not that God hated Esau beyond the possibility of repentance, but that *"God resists the proud, but gives grace to the humble"* (1 Peter 5:5). Also, bringing to remembrance the words of David, he writes, *"I hate them with perfect hatred; I count them my enemies"* (Psalms 139:22), and again in David's own repentance, he explains his perfect hatred, *"Restore to me the joy of Your salvation, and uphold me by Your generous Spirit. Then I will teach transgressors Your ways, and sinners shall be converted to You"* (Psalms 51:12–13).

Considering our worth as living saints, it is incorrect for us to primarily look to the saints of old for our prayers and petitions to our Holy Father or look to the blessed and holy mother Mary to whom our Lord says, "Woman, *behold your son*" and to the beloved disciple, *"Behold your mother."* Assuredly, I say to you that we are the beloved disciples and saints of Jesus Christ if we are given to Him, wholly set apart to grace and given to good works, that we may inherit glory according to righteous judgment. But concerning the angels, God has spoken, and proved through divine witness of Apostle Paul, the scripture of Enoch *"Go, say to the Watchers of heaven, who have sent thee to pray for them, you ought to pray for men, and not men for you."* Considering the words of Christ, *"For in the resurrection they neither marry nor are given in marriage, but are like angels of God in heaven"* (Matthew 22:30). Inasmuch as the scripture speaks, the heavenly saints and angels do in fact make intercession for the earthly saints, whether we ask of them or according to the heavenly will, just as even Christ our Lord makes intercession for us. Of these things, concerning the prayers of those present with the Lord, it is written by Saint Luke, as the woman is shouting, *"Blessed* is *the womb that bore You, and the breasts which nursed You!"* (Luke 11:27). To this, our Lord rebutted, *"More than that, blessed are those who hear the word of God and keep it!"* (Luke 11:28). Or does a child need to call to his brother or mother in order to make a petition for himself? Nonetheless, remember the words of Elijah to Elisha. Difficult things may need an extra petition or intercession. Those in heaven, being absent from the body and present with the Lord, are still alive in Christ; and they being passed are truly alive, whereas those who dwell on the earth until the Lord's return are still being sown in corruption. Those saints, being in glory, have a pure voice in heaven to grace the ears of our God in His spiritual domain. Yet all who believe in the Son of God and confess Him shall be mysteriously raised into incorruption to rule and reign with Christ in the flesh as sons of light.

As I have already shown you, it is not right for men to pray for angels, but angels for men. We are married to Christ as His holy bride, set apart and consecrated, and He is our bridegroom indeed. Until the resurrection of the saints in those last days, they are merely born of spirit in our Lord and not yet glorified in their flesh before Christ. They being *"like angels"* are not angels but temporarily ordained spiritual beings. As it is written, *"We are confident, yes, well pleased rather to be absent from the body and to be present with the Lord"* (2 Corinthians 5:8). Therefore, it is not the same as speaking to another brother alive in the flesh and alive in the spirit simultaneously, seeing as to how they (the saints of old) are dead in the flesh. Therefore, let us not fall into the same folly as King Saul seeking Samuel. Assuredly, I say to you that the greater wine is brought forth last once men are well drunk. Assuredly, I say unto you, that wine is well fermented and perfected over time. What is it that the wine of the sudden second coming of our Lord has fermented since His first coming? Saint James, the brother of our Lord, has this to say, *"But let patience have its perfect work, that you may be perfect and complete, lacking nothing"* (James 1:4). Assuredly, I say to you that when men drink the wine pressed from them in their youth, they receive it with joy; but when the blood of Christ (the wine) is placed in the new wineskins of younger men, those older wineskins burst upon contact. These men then say to themselves, *"The old is better"* (Luke 5:39). They do not immediately desire the new, nor do they realize things pertaining to the spirit and view their own life's wine instead of that of our Lord. The Preacher of Ecclesiastes says, *"Do not say to yourself 'why were the former days better than these' for you do not inquire wisely"* (Ecclesiastes 7:10). Assuredly, I say to you that our Lord tells us, *"Blessed is he who does not see, yet still believes"* (John 20:29). We all have been placed on the earth for such a time as this, for *"There is a time to be born and a time to die"* (Ecclesiastes 3:2).

The Lord came to His disciples, knowing first that they (having Him there in the flesh) would produce great fishers of men for in Him is preeminence over all things. Jesus said that *"no flesh would be saved"* unless He comes quickly and cuts off the end-time trials and persecutions. Of this matter, Jesus says, *"Gather up the fragments that remain, so that nothing is lost"* (John 6:12). Of Him, to Him, and through Him have all things been made. Without Him, nothing was made that was made. Therefore, let us rejoice in the Lord our God that He gives not the Spirit by measure, and all things have been given to Christ Jesus from heaven above. Jesus, the only begotten Son of God, took on flesh that the sons of men might have God's given authority over all things. For these things are written in Matthew's

Gospel after He forgives and then heals the paralytic, "*They marveled and glorified God, who had given such power to men*" (Matthew 9:8). These things are affirmed by Saint John in his gospel, "*So Jesus said to them again, 'Peace to you! As the Father has sent Me, I also send you.' And when He had said this, He breathed on them, and said to them, 'Receive the Holy Spirit. If you forgive the sins of any, they are forgiven them; if you retain the sins of any, they are retained'*" (John 20:22–23). And to Saint Peter in Matthew's Gospel, "*And I will give you the keys of the kingdom of heaven, and whatever you bind on earth will be bound in heaven, and whatever you lose on earth will be loosed in heaven*" (Matthew 16:19).

How great that our Lord repeats this glorious thing yet again not just to Peter, but also to all of His disciples! Let us, therefore, maintain a healthy respect for the saints of old, the blessed and holy mother Mary, and revere those who wrote the New Testament. Just as they were men (as was Christ), so are we. Jesus says this (and so let it be), "*Every scribe instructed concerning the kingdom of heaven is like a householder who brings out of his treasure things new and old*" (Matthew 13:52), "*I am the God of Abraham, the God of Isaac, and the God of Jacob. God is not the God of the dead, but of the living*" (Matthew 22:32), and "*I have sent you to reap that for which you have not labored; others have labored, and you have entered into their labors*" (John 4:38). Rejoice for we serve a living God! The life eternal in Him has manifested itself to us in this life that we may partake of His divine cup everlasting in the kingdom of God. Let it be as Saint Paul the apostle says, "*Indeed, let God be true but every man a liar*" (Romans 3:4). Praise God that I have not the final word, but His holy apostles of old do, who He preordained to carry God's word by the Spirit of promise; of which we are all sealed with righteousness, testifying of the Son; keeping the will our heavenly Father in our hearts as tablets of flesh.

Of the reading of the Holy Scriptures, which cannot be broken, is it possible that they should be read in the flesh without the veil being removed or, if you will, the temple torn? Perhaps you know better than the Spirit of our Father. Assuredly, I say to you that what is born of flesh is flesh and what is born of spirit is of the spirit. He who comes from above is greater than that which is of the earth. Therefore, let the old things pass away and become new in Christ Jesus and His holy covenant, by His blood and His flesh, which was shed and broken for all. Therefore, the new is greater than the old. What is old was given by an angel of God, but now what is it that we have had God take on flesh to appear before men and bear the burden of sin upon Himself? All things of old are written to the glory and purpose of Christ, and for Him are their sole purpose. Let us take, for example, these things written in Ecclesiastes:

> *"I returned and saw under the sun that—the race is not to the swift, nor the battle to the strong, Nor bread to the wise, nor riches to men of understanding, nor favor to men of skill; but time and chance happen to them all. For man also does not know his time: like fish taken in a cruel net, like birds caught in a snare, So the sons of men are snared in an evil time, when it falls suddenly upon them."* (Ecclesiastes 9:11–12)

Now consider these things as being under the covenant of Christ and bound as slaves to Him according to righteousness, Him knowing all things has revealed these things by His Spirit in us to us, now being called sons of God. Considering the race, are we not made perfect in our patience? Or of the battle, that in our weakness the strength of Christ is perfected? What of the riches? The Father revealed His Son to babes and not to the prudent. The Lord makes wise the simple. God humbles the exalted and exalts the humble. Perhaps the fear of the Lord is not the beginning of all knowledge, wisdom, and understanding? What of favor? These things are written by Luke in his second book, *"Now when they saw the boldness of Peter and John, and perceived that they were uneducated and untrained men, they marveled. And they realized that they had been with Jesus"* (Acts 4:13). Paul writes to the Corinthians, *"But God has chosen the foolish things of the world to put to shame the wise, and God has chosen the weak things of the world to put to shame the things which are mighty; and the base things of the world and the things which are despised God has chosen, and the things which are not, to bring to nothing the things that are, that no flesh should glory in His presence"* (1 Corinthians 1:27–29). What of death? Perhaps Peter did not know when he would put away his tent or perhaps Paul did not write to Timothy, *"For I am already being poured out as a drink offering, and the time of my departure is at hand. I have fought the good fight, I have finished the race, I have kept the faith. Finally, there is laid up for me the crown of righteousness, which the Lord, the righteous Judge, will give to me on that Day, and not to me only but also to all who have loved His appearing?"* (1 Timothy 4:6–8). Know this, he who seeks shall find, and whoever knocks, to him it will be opened.

Therefore, let us hunger and thirst for righteousness that we may be filled, but let this be the end of the matter. Christ said, *"It is finished."* Of these things, Christ did speak in a less precise yet more accurate manner, driving the purpose of the Ecclesiastical proverb to an end, saying, *"For He makes His sun rise on the evil and on the good, and sends rain on the just and on the unjust"* (Matthew 5:45). Paul says to Corinth, *"We prophesy in part and know in part"* (1 Corinthians 13:9). Let it be known to us that Christ is the bread to the wise. All men are made able to partake of these things. Did Christ not know how He was to be glorified or of what cup He was willing to partake? All things have been given to the Son by the Father, and the Spirit is not given by measure. Therefore, let the Bread of Life be to all men as our common salvation is apparent to all men, and the reading of the scriptures be of Christ and by the Spirit alone. If the scriptures be not interpreted by the Holy Spirit of God, the word is to understanding as Boötes void is to itself: a few wandering lights amidst a sea of darkness, as it is written by the prophet Isaiah, *"The whole vision has become to you like the words of a book that is sealed, which* men *deliver to one who is literate, saying, 'Read this, please.' And he says, 'I cannot, for it is sealed.' Then the book is delivered to one who is illiterate, saying, 'Read this, please.' And he says, 'I am not literate'"* (Isaiah 29:11–12).

God's word is this in 2 Peter 1:20, *"No prophecy of Scripture is of any private interpretation, for prophecy never came by the will of man, but holy men of God spoke as they were moved by the Holy Spirit."*

According to John 1:1, 3–4, *"In the beginning was the Word, and the Word was with God, and the Word was God... All things were made through Him, and without Him nothing was made that was made. In Him was life, and the life was the light of men."* John 1:14 sates, *"The Word became flesh and dwelt among us, and we beheld His glory, the glory as of the only begotten of the Father, full of grace and truth."* Isaiah 55:11 notes, *"So shall My word be that goes forth from My mouth; It shall not return to Me void, but it shall accomplish what I please, and it shall prosper in the thing for which I sent it."* Luke 4:42–43 says, *"Now when it was day, He departed and went into a deserted place. And the crowd sought Him and came to Him, and tried to keep Him from leaving them; but He said to them, 'I must preach the kingdom of God to the other cities also, because for this purpose I have been sent.'"* In Revelation 19:10, it says, *"For the testimony of Jesus is the spirit of prophecy."* Paul writes, *"That you may learn in us not to think beyond what is written"* (1 Corinthians 4:6). Lastly, John writes in his grand Revelation 22:18–19, *"For I testify to everyone who hears the words of the prophecy of this book: If anyone adds to these things, God will add to him the plagues that are written in this book; and if anyone takes away from the words of the book of this prophecy, God shall take away his part from the Book of Life, from the holy city, and from the things which are written in this book."*

The Word of God is the flesh of God that we may consume it, and it lives in us. The drink, which is His blood, is the reality of His greatness and mercy. King David writes, *"Righteousness and justice are the foundation of Your throne; Mercy and truth go before Your face"* (Psalm 89:14). Let us know that the love that God has for us cannot be broken for *"He is love."* Therefore, since the love of God cannot be broken, neither can His word. Our Lord states according to Saint John the beloved, *"The Scripture cannot be broken"* (John 10:35). God's Word was in fact broken, inasmuch as the Word is the bread, which was broken for us. And His mercy was released (which is Christ's blood). These events cut us loose from the curse of the law and brought us from death into everlasting life. For the Word is food indeed for Christ says, *"Man shall not live by bread alone, but by every word that proceeds from the mouth of God"* (Matthew 4:4). So let it not be that any man take scripture to be of personal affection, but instead know it as the glory of Christ. Just as He was glorified in His death and resurrection, He was manifested to us in the flesh unto the glory of God. Let us instead take scripture to be good for personal edification for the glory of our Father in heaven who sees us in secret.

The Word was in fact broken. God became sin. He experienced God-forsakenness. It is written, *"And about the ninth hour Jesus cried out with a loud voice, saying, 'Eli, Eli, lama sabachthani?' that is, 'My God, My God, why have You forsaken Me?'"* (Matthew 27:46). He defeated the grave so that the scripture should not be broken (yet necessary for it to first be broken), for *"And when He had given thanks, He broke it and said, 'Take, eat; this is My body which is broken for you; do this in remembrance of Me.'"* (1 Corinthians 11:24) and *"I am the bread which came down from heaven"* (John 6:42).

> *"Then He said to them, 'These are the words which I spoke to you while I was still with you, that all things must be fulfilled which were written in the Law of Moses and the Prophets and the Psalms concerning Me.' And He opened their understanding, that they might comprehend the Scriptures. Then He said to them, 'Thus it is written, and thus it was necessary for the Christ to suffer and to rise from the dead the third day, and that repentance and remission of sins should be preached in His name to all nations, beginning at Jerusalem.'"* (Luke 24:44–47)

I dare say that there be no greater mystery, especially of God, than that which took place on the hill called Golgotha nearly two thousand years ago, the necessary price to be paid for salvation. Man owed a debt too great to repay, so God paid a debt He did not owe, placing us in even greater debt to Him. Yet we are forgiven of all debt for it is written, *"Therefore I say to you, her sins, which are many, are forgiven, for she loved much. But to whom little is forgiven, the same loves little"* (Luke 7:47). This allows God's creation to love Him forever, always repaying a debt never paid yet fully forgiven, caught up in everlasting gratefulness, being one with the Son as He is with the Father as we are with each other, preserved in Him forevermore, and in communion with one another, creator and created. *"And this is eternal life, that they may know You, the only true God, and Jesus Christ whom You have sent"* (John 17:3). Amen.

Chapter 8

THIS IS THE CONFIDENCE that we have in Jesus that His person truly is the Christ of God; the Christ, the Son of God. And the Son of God *is* God. *"Jesus said to him, 'It is written again, "You shall not tempt the Lord your God"'"* (Matthew 4:7). This is the first proclamation of Jesus' own mouth not only as the Son of the Most High God, but that He is in fact the Most High God. Do not be deceived. God tempts no man, but Satan originates iniquity. So in Christ, we have hope for He who has no sin was tempted by he who fell. It's proof of Satan's perdition and a divine proof of God's holy and wholly consecrated priesthood. It is written in Hebrews 4:15–16, *"For we do not have a High Priest who cannot sympathize with our weaknesses, but was in all points tempted as we are, yet without sin. Let us therefore come boldly to the throne of grace, that we may obtain mercy and find grace to help in time of need."* Just as C. S. Lewis spoke of the Lord's temptations, I paraphrase, who can know the true gravity or force that sin has except He who never succumbed to its shallow desires. Our Lord not only stood in the wind, but He marched against it. However, we lie down in the field or allow ourselves to be driven according to the ease of the wind.

Praise be to God and His holy Lamb that was slain for the sake of the world that we may not have to die in our sins, but be reconciled by grace and saved through faith. To God be all the glory, power, honor, and majesty forevermore. Amen.

It is fitting that such new life in Christ should be brought down into the waters of death (symbolically known as Egypt) and rise again that we may be born both of water and the blood of Christ. So instead of being flooded physically as in Noah's day (the first baptism), we are flooded by His presence (His blood). From us should come rivers of living water, springing forth fountains of life to all men, as it was when Christ was stabbed that water and blood came forth. Saint Paul speaks of these things in his holy epistle to the Romans, *"Or do you not know that as many of us as were baptized into Christ Jesus were baptized into His death? Therefore, we were buried with Him through baptism into death, that just as Christ was raised from the dead by the glory of the Father, even so we also should walk in newness of life"* (Romans 6:3–4). This is the trifold witness on earth before God: the blood, the water, and the Word. Before Satan, there is the lust of the eyes, the lust of the flesh, and the pride of life. Because of the deluge of God, we are wholly born again, fulfilling all righteousness and defeating death and Hades. As our Lord says in Matthew 3:15, *"Permit it to be so now, for thus it is fitting for us to fulfill all righteousness."* Was Christ unrighteous before His baptism? Certainly not! He bathed the Son of Man into God's new man. For by the Law of Moses sin had the advantage, but under grace, the conscience is cleansed, *"For as by one man's disobedience many were made sinners, so also by one Man's obedience many will be made righteous"* (Romans 4:19) and *"The sting of death is sin, and the strength of sin is the law"* (1 Corinthians 15:56).

If even the righteousness of our great and holy King of kings was made complete by the dipping of the body, then how much more us, being sinners, should we fulfill this righteousness? So we are baptized in the name of Christ Jesus, the Son of God, sitting at the right hand of power, eternally glorified and ratified by the Father, and His Holy Spirit, by no other name under heaven other than the one and only true living God. Some say as much as Paul does in 1 Corinthians 1:12–13, *"Now I say this, that each of you says, 'I am of Paul,' or 'I am of Apollos,' or 'I am of Cephas,' or 'I am of Christ.' Is Christ divided? Was Paul crucified for you? Or were you baptized in the name of Paul?"* These things ought not be so.

Whether you be Catholic, Methodist, Baptist, Lutheran, Pentecostal, Orthodox, Presbyterian, or anything else, we are all the body of our Lord Jesus Christ. We should accept any brother, no matter where their affiliation lies in the politics of the church, as a brother in Christ and as a fellow son of the Most High God. So rejoice, brethren! Yes, rejoice for men die and are born again! We were once blind but now see! We were numbered with the transgressors, but now with God! These were dead to righteousness and slaves to sin, yet now are slaves to righteousness and dead to their sins! Let us sing "Halleluiah" to the King of kings and Lord of lords! Let us sing "Holy is the Lamb who was slain!" Let us sing "Holy, holy, holy, Lord God Almighty, who was and is and is to come!" Let us rejoice and be glad in the revelation of Jesus Christ forever and ever! Amen.

Chapter 9

SEEING AS TO HOW we have been born again, let not our speech be worthy of condemnation. Instead, be perfect in all your speech, just as Christ is and was perfect. It is written, *"And as He said these things to them, the scribes and the Pharisees began to assail Him vehemently, and to cross-examine Him about many things, lying in wait for Him, and seeking to catch Him in something He might say, that they might accuse Him"* (Luke 11:53–54). Not being able to find fault in Him, the scripture adds, *"And no one was able to answer Him a word, nor from that day on did anyone dare question Him anymore"* (Matthew 22:46). Paul writes to Titus about those young men, saying, *"Sound speech that cannot be condemned, that one who is an opponent may be ashamed, having nothing evil to say of you"* (Titus 2:8). Because we know that men who practice religion with an unbridled tongue, his religion is useless. James, the brother of Christ, wrote about this in his holy epistle. Saint John says in Revelation 14:20, *"And the winepress was trampled outside the city, and blood came out of the winepress, up to the horses' bridles."* With an agreeable testimony, Saint James first said, *"For we all stumble in many things. If anyone does not stumble in word, he is a perfect man, able also to bridle the whole body. Indeed, we put bits in horses' mouths that they may obey us, and we turn their whole body"* (James 3:2–3). Saint Paul writes to the church of Ephesus, *"Let no corrupt word proceed out of your mouth, but what is good for necessary edification, that it may impart grace to the hearers. And do not grieve the Holy Spirit of God, by whom you were sealed for the day of redemption. Let all bitterness, wrath, anger, clamor, and evil speaking be put away from you, with all malice. And be kind to one another, tenderhearted, forgiving one another, even as God in Christ forgave you"* (Ephesians 4:29–32).

Are we not justly warned by Saint Paul? He wrote to the Galatians, the Romans, and to Timothy (just to name a few) that if we practice the works of the flesh, we will not reap the kingdom of God. Christ said in Matthew 7:26–27, *"But everyone who hears these sayings of Mine, and does not do them, will be like a foolish man who built his house on the sand: and the rain descended, the floods came, and the winds blew and beat on that house; and it fell. And great was its fall."* At the end of the matter, He will say, *"I never knew you; depart from Me, you who practice lawlessness"* (Matthew 7:23). Therefore, do not cast off the new man and do keep that holy thing, which is good and centered in Christ Jesus. It is written by Saint Luke concerning the tongue and righteousness:

> *"Now it happened as they went that He entered a certain village; and a certain woman named Martha welcomed Him into her house. And she had a sister called Mary, who also sat at Jesus' feet and heard His word. But Martha was distracted with much serving, and she approached Him and said, 'Lord, do You not care that my sister has left me to serve alone? Therefore, tell her to help me.' And Jesus answered and said to her, 'Martha, Martha, you are worried and troubled about many things. But one thing is needed, and Mary has chosen that good part, which will not be taken away from her.'"*
> (Luke 10:38–42)

Jesus said to His disciples during the anointing at Bethany by Saint Matthew:

> *"A woman came to Him having an alabaster flask of very costly fragrant oil, and she poured it on His head as He sat at the table. But when His disciples saw it, they were indignant, saying, 'Why this*

waste? For this fragrant oil might have been sold for much and given to the poor.' But when Jesus was aware of it, He said to them, 'Why do you trouble the woman? For she has done a good work for Me. For you have the poor with you always, but Me you do not have always.'" (Matthew 26:7–11)

Chapter 10

Now the gospel message of Christ Jesus is that the Son of God should be manifest from God's word. As His Word in the flesh, He became the mediator for all sin and became sin that we may not sin. It is written in David's psalm that the Lord's word is exalted above His own name. What a great honor it is that we should be called children of God! Now preach no other message than that which Christ and His disciples brought. If any man or angel brings another gospel message, let him be accursed. How great a message is the gospel that even the Lord Himself, when He ascended the mountain to be transfigured before His disciples, spoke of His own death and resurrection that would shortly take place and have it before such great men as Moses and Elijah!

To Enoch was the title king of kings ascribed to, as the kings of the earth asked for him to be their king. Melchizedek was given the title of priest and king. He was the king of Salem. Our father of faith and patriarch gave a tenth of his spoil to him, and he broke bread and poured wine for Abram. Enoch was taken *"for he was not"* (Genesis 5:24). Just as he ascended to heaven to be with the Lord, Jesus also had His own flesh glorified in His ascension (both from the grave and from the earth) to heaven. These men served as signs for the things that would come. Nonetheless, to God be all the glory!

Saint Paul wrote to the Corinthians in his first letter concerning the Old Testament, *"Now all these things happened to them as examples, and they were written for our admonition, upon whom the ends of the ages have come"* (1 Corinthians 10:11). Know that Christ Jesus is the perfect will of God and our Father in heaven. From dust we were born, but He trades beauty for ashes and makes us whiter than snow. To all things, Christ has the preeminence. To Him is all the glory since before the foundations of the world to the end of the age, and His coming in the flesh atop the clouds amidst the cloud of witnesses. To any man who brings another doctrine than that of the exclusivity of Christ Jesus, His coming in the flesh and having come in the flesh, *"do not receive him into your house nor greet him; for he who greets him shares in his evil deeds"* (2 John 1:10–11).

The things written in this *Little Book* are purposed toward the reconciliation of the denominations in Christ Jesus, the Lord of heaven and earth. The things that I have collaborated with the Holy Spirit of our Father should be made known to the brethren. The sin in our hearts and the indoctrination upon our lips indeed sit bitter in the stomach though they are sweet to the tongue, just as John writes in the grand book of the Revelation of Jesus Christ.

> *"Then the voice which I heard from heaven spoke to me again and said, 'Go, take the little book which is open in the hand of the angel who stands on the sea and on the earth.' So I went to the angel and said to him, 'Give me the little book.' And he said to me, 'Take and eat it; and it will make your stomach bitter, but it will be as sweet as honey in your mouth.' Then I took the little book out of the angel's hand and ate it, and it was as sweet as honey in my mouth. But when I had eaten it, my stomach became bitter."* (Revelation 10:8–10)

I proclaim reality (which has itself written a sort of manifesto, even upon ourselves, declaring and proclaiming the faithfulness, justice, and mercy of God), reason, truth, love, logic, and overall preeminence of Christ in all things that all things forevermore be unto the Lord my God—first, the saints; second, the angels in heaven; third, the beasts and fish; and lastly, to inanimate matter. In nature's harmony, it cries out in worship to Christ Jesus for whom it was made. For the same one that gives life everlasting also reserves everlasting chains for those wicked and lazy servants and those unwilling to *"bear fruits worthy of repentance"* (Matthew 3:8) for *"the axe is laid to the root"* (Matthew 3:10).

I bring no other doctrine than that which has been preached since Christ, but only that the kingdom of heaven is at hand and for us to love one another. Therefore, let us all trim our wicks and crucify ourselves, including all our passions and desires, for our first love must be restored before our Lord's second coming. Let us prepare His way in this world, as John the Baptist prepared for His first coming. It is written by the prophet Malachi, *"Behold, I will send you Elijah the prophet before the coming of the great and dreadful day of the Lord. And he will turn the hearts of the fathers to the children, and the hearts of the children to their fathers, lest I come and strike the earth with a curse"* (Malachi 4:5–6). We are the testimony of Jesus and the spirit of prophecy; therefore, let us prophesy the coming of our Lord and hasten His return. It is proper for us then to do the works of John the Baptist. But how much greater are the works of Christ and the Father's Holy Spirit living inside of us than that of the ministry of John the Baptist and the mantle of Elijah?

Let us, therefore, go in the way of Jesus, the Son of the Most High God, and fear Him. It is written by Saint Luke, the beloved physician, from the mouth of the Savior, *"And I say to you, My friends, do not be afraid of those who kill the body, and after that have no more that they can do. But I will show you whom you should fear: Fear Him who, after He has killed, has power to cast into hell; yes, I say to you, fear Him!"* (Luke 12:4–5). I tell you now as Paul wrote to Titus, a true son of the faith, concerning the remission of sins and the hope of eternal glory and everlasting life with the Lord our God:

> *"Remind them to be subject to rulers and authorities, to obey, to be ready for every good work, to speak evil of no one, to be peaceable, gentle, showing all humility to all men. For we ourselves were also once foolish, disobedient, deceived, serving various lusts and pleasures, living in malice and envy, hateful and hating one another. But when the kind-*

ness and the love of God our Savior toward man appeared, not by works of righteousness which we have done, but according to His mercy He saved us, through the washing of regeneration and renewing of the Holy Spirit, whom He poured out on us abundantly through Jesus Christ our Savior, that having been justified by His grace we should become heirs according to the hope of eternal life." (Titus 3:1–7)

Now I, Austin, bid good tidings and great measures of love, joy, peace, understanding, and longsuffering unto you, my fellow saints and laborers in the gospel. Amen. Deep unto deep, grace to grace, glory to glory, and honor and majesty to the King of heaven and of earth forevermore. Amen and amen.

About the Author

ZEALOUS FOR THE TRADITIONS of our fathers before us, I (Austin Winchester) will continue in the wisdom God has given, but never at the expense of a broken and contrite heart. Hearken unto righteousness and the holiness, which belongs to the Lord of hosts. But what is man that God should consider him? God, have mercy on me, a sinner!

CPSIA information can be obtained
at www.ICGtesting.com
Printed in the USA
BVHW040025220423
662811BV00002B/472